AUTISM
THROUGH A SISTER'S EYES

A Book For Children About High-functioning
Autism and Related Disorders

Eve B. Band, Ph.D. and Emily Hecht

Illustrations by Sue Lynn Cotton

FUTURE HORIZONS INC.

721 W. Abram Street
Arlington, Texas 76013

817-277-0727
800-489-0727
817-277-2270 (fax)

E-mail: info@FutureHorizons-autism.com
Homepage: www.FutureHorizons-autism.com

ISBN #1-885477-71-6

PREFACE

Awareness of autism is on the rise as greater numbers of individuals are identified with disorders on the autism spectrum. This book dedicates its primary focus to siblings— the children whose daily lives include a brother or sister with high-functioning autism or Asperger's Syndrome. It is our hope that parents and children will read this book together. Foremost, it is intended for use with siblings for the purpose of providing accurate information specifically about high-functioning autism and related disorders. Second, it is intended to promote discussion about feelings and experiences that are shared by many siblings such as anger, frustration, embarrassment, a sense of responsibility, caring and pride. At the conclusion of the book, questions to facilitate parent-child discussion are included for this purpose.

Because growing numbers of children with high-functioning autism and Asperger's Syndrome are in inclusive school settings, there is also a need for materials to teach about high-functioning autism to classmates and peers. If non-disabled peers learn about high-functioning autism and Asperger's Syndrome, we may improve their sensitivity and understanding in their roles as classmates, friends and peer mentors. The material in this book is appropriate for use by educators, therapists or other professionals.

This is a highly personal book. Although it is written by Eve Band, Ph.D., a clinical psychologist, it gives voice to the actual thoughts, feelings and experiences of Emily Hecht, the nine year old sibling of a brother with high-functioning autism. Based on extensive interviews and discussion with Emily, her parents, and her brother Daniel, the narrative represents Emily's unique viewpoint of her brother's autism. The factual information about autism has been provided by Dr. Band in a form geared toward easy comprehension by children. To this end, no theoretical distinction has been made between high-functioning autism and Asperger's Syndrome, despite ongoing discussion among experts as to whether Asperger's Syndrome is a form of very high-functioning autism or actually represents a distinct disorder.

Our focus has broadened from more severe forms of autism to include wider recognition of milder forms of autistic disorders. It is the authors' most fundamental hope that this book may help others, especially those who live and work with persons with high-functioning autism or Asperger's Syndrome. Writing the book has helped us not only to focus on the challenges about Daniel, but also to celebrate his many strengths and gifts. If others can derive increased knowledge, sensitivity or emotional support from this work, then the product will have been well worth the effort.

AUTHOR ACKNOWLEDGMENT

There are many individuals I would like to thank for their contributions to this book. I am indebted to my husband and children, Steven, Anna and Rebecca, for their patience and understanding. I am grateful to the Hecht family, David, Beth, Emily and Daniel, for their participation and support, without which the book would not have been possible. Coming to know them has been a special gift.

I would also like to thank Wayne Gilpin and Polly McGlew of Future Horizons for their efforts in reviewing and publishing, and Sue Lynn Cotton for her beautifully rendered illustrations. Those who generously provided thoughtful comments on the manuscript include Gary Mesibov, Ph.D., Lynn Medley, CCC-SLP, Elaine Williams, M.A., Steven Band, Ph.D., and David Band, M.D. I am also appreciative of the support and encouragement of Ellen Gillette, Wendy Gelber, Kathy Lopez and Lisa Band.

Finally, I would like to acknowledge the parents and children whose daily lives include a family member with autism or Asperger's syndrome, whom I have come to know through my professional practice. Truly, this book is dedicated to them, and I am grateful for the inspiration and enriched understanding they have contributed to my work.

Eve Band

FAMILY ACKNOWLEDGMENT

There are many special people that we would like to thank for their inspiration and support. Helping to write this book has been a gratifying and enriching process for us. It has helped us to look at our life as a family and the joys and challenges we face daily.

There have been many wonderful teachers, specialists and therapists who have helped to guide our journey with Daniel. A constant source of strength has been the close circle of friends and family whose love and concern motivated us to move forward on this project. This book is a way for us to show our appreciation and to give something back to them.

We want to especially acknowledge Dr. Eve Band. She has given our family essential information, support and direction for many years. A special thank you to Dr. Steven Band for his patience while this book took on a life of its own over these many months.

Beth, David, Daniel, and Emily Hecht

FOREWORD

Having an opportunity to work with students like Eve Band are what I love about my job. I met Eve years ago when she was a graduate student and then a Clinical Psychology Intern at the University of North Carolina at Chapel Hill. I always looked forward to our supervision sessions because Eve was so thoughtful and interesting. What I remember best from those years we worked so closely together were her creativity, insight, sensitivity, and splendid writing skills. Surprisingly little has changed since she left Chapel Hill over a decade ago because those are the hallmarks of this book and the reason why anyone who reads it will be captivated.

Eve's creativity and unique way of looking at situations has helped her find a fascinating approach for this book. One of her clients, Emily Hecht, was confronting the many complex issues facing a sibling of a child with autism. Eve started to write this book with Emily as a part of their sessions together and the process helped both of them to articulate and deal with many of the thoughts and conflicts that concern siblings. During this process Eve recognized the rare and special ideas they were generating together and with Emily's and her family's permission helped organize their insights into this wonderful book.

The book combines a nine-year-old's remarkable natural sensitivity with a seasoned professional's organization and thoughtful conceptualizations. The result is a very special combination.

It is always a great joy and privilege to work with students like Eve but quite sad when they leave, as they inevitably do, to make their mark on the world. The sadness passes as I maintain contact with them and see how they grow and develop. With Eve this sadness has evolved into a feeling of great pride and satisfaction seeing products like this book and feeling that I played a part, however small, in its overall development. It is very reassuring for me to realize that others will now know of Eve's and her collaborator's special insights and talents as many read, enjoy, and learn from this remarkable book.

Gary B. Mesibov, Ph.D.

Professor and Director
Division TEACCH
Department of Psychiatry
University of North Carolina at Chapel Hill

CONTENTS

INTRODUCTION

I was first asked to evaluate Daniel Hecht in 1995 when I was working as a consultant to the Baltimore County Public Schools Autism/PDD program. He was six years old and it was requested that I assess his level of cognitive functioning and clarify his original diagnosis of "PDD-NOS" (Pervasive Developmental Disorder, Not Otherwise Specified). Four years later, when Daniel was close to turning eleven, the Hecht family returned to me for further services for Daniel and indicated that they also wanted me to see his younger sister, Emily, then aged nine. They explained that they wanted to increase her understanding of her brother and his autism.

When Emily came to see me for her first session, she brought with her a copy of a book written for children about autism, which described the world of a classically autistic child and his family. As we looked at this book together, I asked her if she saw anything of her own feelings or experiences with her brother, Daniel. As Emily shook her head indicating that she saw little similarity, I promised her that I would try to locate something for us to read together that was more relevant to her experiences with a brother with high-functioning autism.

The next time Emily came to see me I found myself apologizing that my search for something really fitting for us to read together had come up empty handed. It was then that I suggested to Emily that we would "write our own book" describing her firsthand experiences, and, contrasting "classic" autism with higher-functioning autism and Asperger's Syndrome to help her learn more about her brother. My aim was solely therapeutic. I envisioned that helping Emily tell her story would provide a vehicle for discussing her feelings as a sibling and understanding new information about high-functioning autism and Asperger's

Syndrome. However, over the course of several more meetings together, Emily and I became increasingly excited about our "project." I was moved and inspired by her articulate descriptions of her life with Daniel. When Emily and I finally read our "book" to her parents (all eight or ten pages of it) no eye remained dry. I remember remarking to her parents, David and Beth, how much a "real" book like this could help other kids like Emily who are the brothers and sisters of children with high-functioning autism or Asperger's Syndrome.

This was how **Through A Sister's Eyes** began. With the Hechts' support and insights, I expanded and developed the story into its present form based on my initial work with Emily, as well as further interviews with Emily and her parents. Deciding to "go public" with the book and reveal Emily and Daniel's actual identities was a lengthy and delicate process. I truly admire Emily's courage in wanting to reach out to other children who also are siblings with a family member with high-functioning autism or Asperger's Syndrome. I hope that Emily's story will enrich your understanding and speak to you in a meaningful way, as it has to me.

Eve B. Band, Ph.D.

CHAPTER ONE

INTRODUCING EMILY

Hello. My name is Emily and I am nine years old. I want to tell you about my eleven year old brother, Daniel. Daniel is autistic. He has a type of autism called *high-functioning autism*, which some people call Asperger's Syndrome. As Daniel's sister, I have had to learn a lot about people with high-functioning autism. I had to learn about what it's like and how to deal with it in my family. Before I learned about autism, it was confusing and hard to understand why my brother seemed different from me and from most other kids I knew. I didn't really know why he often talked out loud to himself, or copied what I said and repeated it right back to me, or flapped his hands in the air when he got excited.

My Mom and Dad tell me I used to ask them, "why does Daniel do that?" whenever he did something kind of weird or funny. But learning about autism and Asperger's Syndrome has really helped me understand my brother a lot better. It has helped me to know why Daniel does some things differently from me and to know how to get along better. I would like to share with you some of the things I have learned. I think that if you have a brother or sister, classmate or other family member with high-functioning autism, learning more about it can help you too.

CHAPTER TWO

GETTING TO KNOW DANIEL

When you look at my brother Daniel, he looks just like

a regular person. You might see that he is very handsome.

He has dark brown hair and hazel eyes, and, just like you

and me, Daniel has two eyes,

two ears, two arms and

legs, and he walks,

runs, talks, eats

and plays. If you

saw Daniel and me

walking down the

street or saw us

outside playing ball,

you probably would not be able

to tell that he has autism or that he is any different from you and me. But if you stayed nearby and spent more time around Daniel you might begin to notice some things about him that are different from most other boys his age.

Sometimes Daniel just starts talking out loud to himself. Like we could be in the grocery store or out somewhere and he just starts jabbering away. Or when we play hide and seek, we like to make funny noises; but Daniel keeps on talking even while he's looking for me, so it sounds like he's talking to a ghost or something. Other times he might laugh really loudly at things that aren't funny, even if no one else if laughing. Also, you might see that whenever Daniel leaves our house, he needs to bring a toy or book with him, usually something to do with a movie made by Walt Disney, like the storybook of Snow White or some kind of Disney toy figure. When I was younger, this didn't seem weird to me. Sometimes I carried special toys with me too, when I was little. But I'm nine now and I stopped doing this as I got older. Daniel doesn't know this looks kind of funny at his age even though he is eleven years old.

If you came over and tried to talk to Daniel, he's usually friendly and he would not have any problem telling you his name and age. But he might not be able to tell you his correct address or phone number or give answers to harder questions, and he might not look at you when you and he are talking. And if you asked Daniel something else, like to let you see his Game Boy, he might tell you "no" or say things that don't really make sense. Daniel has a hard time understanding about how his Game Boy works. He thinks that his friend broke his Game Boy because one time, when he was playing, the batteries ran low. Daniel couldn't understand that batteries run low sometimes and this doesn't mean the Game Boy is broken. Now, whenever this friend comes over, Daniel hides his Game Boy so "it won't get broken."

CHAPTER THREE

DANIEL HAS FEELINGS TOO

Sometimes I worry that people who don't know that

Daniel has autism will think he's just really weird. Or I worry

people will tease and make fun of him, like when he laughs

really loudly or says something that doesn't make sense. And

it's also a problem that it's easy to hurt Daniel's feelings.

Usually he doesn't understand when others joke or tease, or

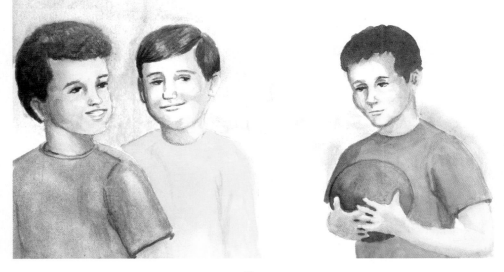

use sarcasm to say things they don't really mean. It is important to remember that people with autism have feelings too. Maybe the next time that you meet someone who seems weird or different, you might want to think if that person has a disability, like autism, and remember that he or she has feelings that can get hurt, just like me and you.

I hope that by telling you about my brother Daniel and explaining what I've learned about his autism it will help you understand and feel more comfortable when you're with kids like my brother. Maybe it will also help you to understand the importance of saying nice things to him and not hurting his feelings. After all, Daniel didn't choose to have autism, just like you and I didn't choose to have Blonde hair or brown hair, or be short or tall. He can't always help it when he acts funny or weird. But he still needs to be liked and accepted by other kids, just like you and I do.

CHAPTER FOUR

FINDING OUT ABOUT AUTISM

When my parents and I met with my brother's doctor, she explained that autism is a problem that begins when children are very young, usually before age three. When a child has autism, you might hear people say that he or she is *"autistic."* Most people say that autism is a type of disability, because kids with autism have problems with talking, playing and learning. Not all autistic children are alike. Some children with autism have lots of severe problems which almost everyone can see. This is usually called *"moderate or severe autism."* But other children with autism have problems that are milder and harder to recognize. This is usually called *"high-functioning autism or Asperger's Syndrome."*

Children do not outgrow or "get rid of" autism as they get older, but, with help, many of their problems can get better. The reason children with autism have problems with how they think, feel and behave is because their brains work differently from yours and mine. Parts of the brain don't work the right way from the time they are born. You can't "catch" autism from someone, like you catch a cold or the flu. Doctors and scientists are working hard to study and learn more about how the brains of persons with autism are different, and to find new ways to help children with autism.

CHAPTER FIVE

MODERATE AND SEVERE AUTISM

First, let me tell you more about *"moderate and severe autism."* Children with moderate or severe autism often have problems learning to talk and learning social skills such as how to make friends, play with others, and understand what other people are saying. Many children with moderate or

severe autism don't like loud noises, bright lights, being touched, or too much excitement. Often, they don't like it so much to be around people and they might become very upset when they are in situations where there are big crowds of people or lots of noise. They might also become upset when things change or aren't the way they like them to be (like if every morning you **always** have Cornflakes for breakfast, but one day you have to have Cheerios because your Mom is out of Cornflakes).

Sometimes severely autistic children like to do unusual things over and over, like rocking back and forth, spinning round and round, or staring at lights. Also, most children with moderate or severe autism don't know how to play like other kids do. Usually, they don't know how to use their imagination to do pretend or "make-believe" play with their toys. Instead, they might spend lots of time lining up their toys in a row, or even putting things in their mouths to see what they feel or taste like.

Many children with moderate or severe autism also have problems learning and learn more slowly than most regular kids. To help them learn, children with moderate or severe autism are often in special classes at school. But a few kids with autism are really, really good at certain things, like music, or numbers, or puzzles, or remembering facts and dates. Although these special skills or talents are *not* very common, a few kids with autism can do amazing things, like figure out number problems in their heads in just seconds!

CHAPTER SIX

LEARNING ABOUT HIGH-FUNCTIONING AUTISM

Now, let me explain more about my brother Daniel and *high-functioning autism*. As I mentioned earlier, Daniel has a milder type of autism called *high-functioning autism* (HFA). Sometimes this is also called *Pervasive Developmental Disorder* (PDD) or *Asperger's Syndrome* (AS) by doctors and other experts. This can be confusing because even though Daniel shows some of the same problems seen in children with moderate or severe autism, his problems are not as bad or obvious. That made it harder for my parents and the doctors to figure out that Daniel had some type of autism (we didn't actually know for sure until he was three years old!). But my Mom and Dad already worried, when he was little, that there was a problem because it took him much longer than most kids to learn to talk and play.

When I was little I didn't know that Daniel was any different from me or other kids. I remember that when I was three years old and he was five we would just play together and have fun. I thought he was still like me. But when I was like six years old, and in the first grade, I started to see that he was different from me. I'm not sure what I felt when I first realized this. I began to wonder why he watched movies and laughed at stuff that wasn't funny, or why he didn't get it at all

when things actually were funny. And sometimes I noticed

that Daniel would just start to giggle for no reason at all. Then

I would start to laugh, and my parents would start to laugh,

and soon we're all laughing for no reason at all!

CHAPTER SEVEN

MAKING FRIENDS AND BEING WITH PEOPLE

My brother Daniel likes to be with me and my family and friends. Sometimes people say that children with autism seem to be lost in their own little world. But Daniel is usually friendly to others and he even has some of his own friends. But it is harder for him to know how to make friends the way I do. Lots of children with *high-functioning autism* want to have

friends, but they have trouble knowing how to make friends and relate to others.

Kids need to know how to do certain things to be able to make friends and get along well with other people. Like, you and I know to look at people when they are talking, how to take turns in a game, or to join a group of kids (maybe by saying, "that looks like fun, can I play too?"). Understanding how to get along with people is often a big problem for children with high-functioning autism. For example, Daniel often forgets to look at people when they are speaking, so sometimes it's hard for others to tell whether he is listening to what they're saying. And Daniel likes to talk mostly about certain things that interest him, like his favorite Disney movies. But often he doesn't remember to ask kids about other things that they like, or talk about different things.

Most kids, like you and I, don't have difficulty understanding how to get along with others. We just learn it naturally, without really thinking so much about it, from being with other people like our family and friends. But Daniel needs help to learn how to get along with people. He has to practice and be taught what to say and do, just the way you and I learn things like math or reading. Because knowing how to have friends and get along with others is really important, Daniel works on this at school, and we help him to practice at home, too.

CHAPTER EIGHT

TALKING AND UNDERSTANDING

Another problem for Daniel is being able to talk and understand things people say the way that other kids do. Problems with language, such as talking and understanding what people are saying, are common for children with autism. Children with *high-functioning autism* can be delayed in starting to talk, but once they do they may actually talk a lot, but often they talk in weird or unusual ways. For

example, Daniel doesn't always know the right words to say, he doesn't use correct grammar the way I do, and he doesn't know the meanings of harder words (like the ones that are on my fourth grade spelling list!).

Also, Daniel likes best to talk about certain topics he really likes, such as anything from Disney (like Disney movies, songs and stories) or his favorite T.V. shows like Arthur or Rugrats. The doctors explained to me that talking a lot about only certain particular subjects is also part of Daniel's autism. I learned that it is common for children with *high-functioning autism* to have "narrow interests." This means having one special thing they are really interested in, like animals, science, weather or computers, and think and talk about it all the time, over and over.

If you ask Daniel to tell you about his favorite book or movie, he will tell you all about something from Disney, like

Sleeping Beauty. It's good to talk with Daniel about his special interests, because then it's easy for him to talk to you. But instead of telling you just a little about it, Daniel will usually go on and on and on telling you every little last detail in the story, even when you don't want to hear any more. It's hard for Daniel to know when to stop talking about something he likes, especially when it's about Disney. It's okay to tell him that he needs to stop when he has gone on too long or if you are in a hurry. Sometimes my Mom and Dad and I have to remind him not to keep on talking about it, or we need to tell him, "that's enough" and that it is time for him to stop, or to talk about something else other than Disney.

Another thing about how Daniel talks and understands language is that he has a hard time knowing what jokes and expressions mean. Children with *high-functioning autism* understand most things we say, but they often "don't get" the more subtle meaning of jokes and expressions the way you and I do. Daniel gets his feelings hurt sometimes because he can't always tell when I'm just kidding around or saying things I don't really mean. And, if I tell a joke, Daniel usually doesn't understand the funny part. Or if I use an expression like, "let's hit the road," Daniel might be confused and think that I actually mean to take a stick and hit the street, instead of understanding that its really a way of saying "let's get going."

When I was learning to read, I loved to read books by author Peggy Parish about the character Amelia Bedelia. I thought these books were so funny because Amelia Bedelia is always making mistakes and doing funny things because she misunderstands what others have said to her. For example, in one book Amelia is told to "dress the chicken" which really means to prepare it for cooking. But she doesn't understand this, so she puts little clothes on the chicken instead! This reminds me of my brother Daniel because sometimes he has trouble figuring out the real meaning of things that people say, just like Amelia Bedelia.

CHAPTER NINE

FUN AND PLAY

Sometimes I like to play with Daniel and we have fun together. The other night we played baseball outside. But when we play together, I know that Daniel often has trouble understanding the rules of the game, or playing the way that you and I like to do. Children with *high-functioning autism* often have problems knowing how to play together with other children. Sometimes they have trouble

knowing how to follow rules in a game and understanding about winning and losing. Also, kids with high-functioning autism often like to do the same exact things again and again and have trouble thinking up new or different ideas of things to do for fun.

You see, when I'm with my friends we like to do all kinds of different things, like board games or arts and crafts. Daniel and his friends usually play the same things over and over again. When Daniel plays with his friends who have autism they usually play video games, watch movies, or play with his Disney action figures. Most often they just pretend to have the action figures fight or they use them to act out scenes they know by memory from television shows and Disney movies. Sometimes, Daniel and his friend don't even play together, but play separately in the same room without talking to each other.

I think that Daniel is happiest when he's watching his favorite movie, playing with his stuffed animals, or playing with his Disney action figures. But I like to try new things and there are all kinds of different things that I like to do for fun. Because of his autism, it is harder for Daniel than it is for me to have a lot of different hobbies or interests, or to think up lots of different ways to play and have fun. It is also harder for Daniel to know how to play together with kids his age, rather than just doing the things he wants to do either alone, or by having others follow his set routines.

Sometimes I try to play games with Daniel, like Nintendo or Monopoly Junior. When we do this Daniel always quits in the middle. We're having a good time and I ask him, "Why do you want to stop? We're having so much fun." Then he says that he just wants to quit. Sometimes Daniel will just start doing weird stuff, and he dozes off into his own little world. Then my Mom or Dad or I say, "earth to

Daniel" and he knows that means to come back and focus again. I think it is hard for Daniel to stick with things and pay attention for a long time like I can do. The exception to this is when he is doing things that involve his special interests or rigid routines. He really sticks with it then, like when he watches the same video for hours at a time, even though he has already seen it many times before.

CHAPTER TEN

DEALING WITH CHANGES

Usually, Daniel is in a pretty good mood. But if his schedule changes he's not happy, especially if he didn't know about the change ahead of time. Many children with autism have trouble coping with unexpected changes, like having to do an errand on the

way home that wasn't planned. Sometimes my Mom needs to make a quick stop for food at the grocery store after she picks us up from school. Daniel often gets upset when this happens. He also gets upset, sometimes, when he is "transitioning" between things and he is finishing one activity and getting ready to start another. When he's not in a good mood or when he's transitioning, even the smallest things bother Daniel. Like if I'm singing along with the car radio, or even if I just look at him, he starts complaining and tells me to stop.

Most children with autism feel the most comfortable when things happen the same way every time. It helps Daniel to have a schedule, so he will know when things are going to happen and what to expect. Daniel is still learning how to deal with it when plans unexpectedly change. This last summer during our family vacation at the Delaware shore, Daniel got sick and so we had to change our plans for spending time at an amusement park on the boardwalk that we really like. Daniel got mad when this happened. I understood that he felt disappointed, but he was really upset.

He got grumpy and started whining, and kept asking the same questions over and over. Daniel gets on my nerves when he acts this way, but I try to remember that this is his way of trying to work through his feelings. Because of his autism, situations like this with unexpected changes are especially hard for Daniel.

CHAPTER ELEVEN

FEELING WORRIED

Another thing, though, about Daniel, is that he worries a lot. Usually, he worries about things that he doesn't really have to worry about. Like if I have to cross the street to get a ball that went into the neighbor's yard. I know to be careful and look both ways before I cross the street, but Daniel gets upset and worries anyway. He always tells me to "watch out." He just doesn't understand if I say it's okay and that you don't have to be worried.

Daniel also worries over and over about other little things. He worries a lot about our dog getting loose, thunderstorms, and losing the electricity or power in our house. Last winter our power went off during bad weather and we were without any electricity for several days. Now almost every time we come home and the lights are off he starts to worry and asks if the power is out. So we have to turn the lights on right away to show him it's okay. Worrying an extra lot about certain things is pretty common in people with high-functioning autism.

In some situations, kids with autism have a lot of trouble with feeling worried, upset, or paying attention. For some children with autism this can be a really big problem that gets in the way of being calm and happy, or listening and learning at school. When he was younger, my parents took Daniel to a special doctor who gave him medicine to help with these problems. Sometimes medicine can be helpful, but it doesn't cure or change autism. Now that Daniel is older he doesn't use the medicine any more. But, some kids need to keep on taking their medicine for many years, to help them with these kinds of problems.

CHAPTER TWELVE

DIFFICULT FEELINGS FOR EMILY

Sometimes it's kind of hard having Daniel as my

brother. There have been times when he has embarrassed

me, made me really mad, or when I've felt worried about him.

Even though I am actually two years younger than he is, there

are times that I feel kind of responsible for Daniel, like if he's

having a problem or might be in a situation where he doesn't know what to do and needs my help.

One summer, when we were both going to day camp, other kids were teasing him. I had to be the one to stand up for him and tell them to stop. I think that if I'm nearby, like going to the same camp, I often start to worry about Daniel. I might think, "oh, is he lost" or things like that. I think that it helps me to be in a separate place of my own sometimes, because then I usually don't think or worry about him as much when I'm supposed to be having fun.

Other times though, Daniel does stuff that makes me feel embarrassed. I know that usually he just doesn't realize it and that he doesn't mean to embarrass me or act weird. One time when I was only seven years old (and he was nine) my Mom was taking me to a friend's house to play. As soon as we got there, Daniel just ran right into her house without asking and started to play. My Mom pulled him out but I still felt that I had to make excuses about his behavior. After all he was nine years old! And when we go to the movies Daniel will laugh really loud, more loudly than other kids are laughing. It's pretty embarrassing, but my Mom always reminds me that it's dark in there and no one in the movie theatre knows it's us.

Probably one of the things that is hardest is when I feel mad and frustrated with Daniel. I know that most all brothers are probably annoying to their sisters, but sometimes Daniel really gets on my nerves. Like today, we were all on our way to an appointment with the doctor and my Mom reminded us that she was going to have to work all day and that we would have a sitter. So Daniel has to ask, "what's all day?" as if he had no idea what she was talking about. I know that he knows what "all day" means, but he just has to ask, anyway.

It's frustrating for me sometimes when Daniel always asks questions, when he already knows the answers. But I've learned that many people with *high-functioning autism* like to ask lots of questions, sometimes even the same ones, over and over again. Even though they already know the answer they feel comforted to hear the same answer again and again.

CHAPTER THIRTEEN

LEARNING TO COPE

Something important I've had to learn, being Daniel's sister, is what to do to help myself with my feelings when I'm mad, upset, worried or frustrated. I've learned that it is okay to have these feelings and that it is perfectly normal to sometimes feel this way. Sometimes when Daniel is bothering me I try to just ignore him. If we're at home, I'll go to

another room and do something else. I try to take my mind off of it so that it doesn't keep bothering me. At other times, especially when he's getting on my nerves, I might try to just walk away. This works best though if I remember to do it before I'm feeling too upset or annoyed, so I can calm down. Another thing I sometimes try to do, is to just stop and think. I remind myself that Daniel usually doesn't mean to bother me. It helps me to remember and tell myself that some of the annoying stuff Daniel says or does is because of his high-functioning autism.

Until recently, I felt kind of embarrassed and worried about what my friends would think about my brother. Daniel and I go to different schools. Before, I didn't really want the kids from my school to know about him. But now I don't worry much about it like I used to. My good friends are nice to Daniel. They like him and accept him just the way he is. It seems that the more time they spend with me when he's around, the more they feel comfortable and understand about him. Even some of my friends' brothers are nice to him and include him in some of their activities. This makes me feel good and it makes Daniel feel great! And if he does something that is funny or weird, that's okay. I know a lot about Daniel's autism now. I can explain why he does certain things if someone asks. I can even help my friends learn about his autism.

Sometimes, though, I just get really mad and frustrated and I don't feel like putting up with Daniel or being understanding. I might want him to stay away from me and my friends, so he doesn't bother us or bug me. I might do things to annoy him back if he's getting on my nerves. Or, I might even be the one who starts it by bothering him, just like all brothers and sisters do some of the time.

Once in a while, I wish that I had a different brother who didn't have autism. I watch other kids with their brothers and sisters and think that it's not fair, he's so annoying, why can't I have a "normal" brother like they do. I feel kind of bad about it when I feel this way. Usually, I don't want to tell anyone. But my Mom and Dad are pretty good at understanding me, even when I'm upset and have these feelings. And Daniel's doctor also explained that other kids have feelings like this too, because it can be pretty hard sometimes having to be understanding and put up with a brother or sister who has special needs. Sometimes I even feel like **I** am the older kid in the family, even though I'm the younger sister and Daniel is two years older than me. It can get frustrating when I feel like I have to be the responsible one.

It has helped me to talk to others who know about autism, like my Mom and Dad, or a doctor, or other kids who also have brothers and sisters who have high-functioning autism like Daniel. I'm lucky that my family is really close and we can talk about our feelings. My parents understand that I feel angry and frustrated sometimes. Everyone feels this way sometimes with their siblings, even if they don't have special needs.

CHAPTER FOURTEEN

FEELING GOOD WITH DANIEL

Even though it is hard to live with Daniel sometimes, there are many good parts about being his sister. Like he makes me laugh and we have fun together. Sometimes Daniel says things that are really funny without even trying to. Other times, Daniel and I love to act out characters from movies. He

remembers all the words from many movies and he can even make himself sound just like the real movie character. He also knows commercials from T.V. Sometimes Daniel can say whole commercials without even taking a breath!

Another good thing is that Daniel is one of the nicest people I know. He is usually smiling and happy and he likes to tell me about his day or something that he finds interesting. Another way Daniel is nice is that he doesn't understand how to be mean. He doesn't go out of his way to try to tease and hurt others' feelings, or be nasty and annoying. Even though he sometimes makes me feel annoyed or upset, he doesn't really mean to. Actually, Daniel often starts to get upset and worried himself if he notices that something is bothering me. Usually, he tries to say something because he wants me to feel better. (Unfortunately, this is when I often think he is the most annoying!)

There are also times when I feel really proud of Daniel. Daniel has his own unique talents, interests and abilities. Some people with *high-functioning autism* are really good at certain things, like computers, geography, drawing, or science. Sometimes kids with high-functioning autism are able to use their special interests to learn all about something or be really good at it. Like Daniel is especially good at spelling and reading at school. He has a good memory and he does very well on his spelling tests. He also especially enjoys music, singing and drama. I think that he has a beautiful voice when he sings. He has also been successful at taking a drama class and participating in plays.

Not too long ago, Daniel's school put on a play. When my Mom, Dad and I went to see him in it I felt really proud of him. He did a scene from the story "101 Dalmatians" and he did a really super job. He knew what he was supposed to say all by memory and everyone could hear him when he did his part! Daniel is also good at using nice manners with other people. Sometimes, when someone gives him something, like a small snack or toy, he thanks them with such enthusiasm, it's as if they had done something extra special.

There's another good part I want to tell you about being Daniel's sister that I only learned about recently. People have always told me I'm a really sensitive kind of kid. Being sensitive means that you're especially good at caring and thinking about other people and their feelings. I had never thought that my being good at caring about what others think and feel had anything to do with me being Daniel's sister. But one of Daniel's doctors pointed out to me that I know much more than most kids my age about how to be sensitive to others, especially to persons who have a disability, because of my growing up with Daniel. I hadn't thought about it like that before. But I feel good about being that kind of person, who thinks and cares about others.

CHAPTER FIFTEEN

LOOKING AHEAD

I've lived with my brother now for nine years and I keep learning more and more about him. I've learned a lot about the way Daniel thinks and feels. And I've learned about how Daniel sometimes acts differently from you and me and most other people. Not many kids I know have a brother or sister with high-functioning autism like Daniel.

Knowing about high-functioning autism has helped me understand my brother better, understand more about my own thoughts and feelings, and explain about it to others. If you have a brother, sister, other family member, classmate or friend with autism, I hope that learning more about it will help you too.

I am glad that Daniel will always be my brother and that I care about him. Daniel is special, just as everyone is special in their very own way. I know that Daniel will not outgrow having autism as we grow older, but I'm still glad that he's my brother and part of my family.

GLOSSARY

autism - is a type of disability. It can vary from mild (or high-functioning) to severe. It usually appears before children are three years old. Children and adults with autism have a problem with parts of their brain which causes them to think, feel and use their body differently from most other people. People do not "get rid of" or outgrow autism, but their problems can get better with help and treatment.

autistic - is a word used to describe the behavior of persons who have autism.

Asperger's Syndrome - is another name used to mean a type of mild or very high-functioning autism. Many people with Asperger's Syndrome are smart and like to talk. They often have problems understanding how to get along with people and doing certain things over and over again.

developmental delay - is when a baby or young child is late to learn a skill (like to talk or to walk) and they don't start doing it until much later than other kids their age. Children with high-functioning autism are often delayed in learning to talk when they are young, but once they start, sometimes they like to talk a lot.

disability - means having a problem or handicap that gets in the way of doing some of the things that most regular people are able to do. Most people think of autism as a type of disability.

echolalia - is when a person repeats back words or phrases that someone else has said. Children with autism often have echolalia when they speak, especially when they are young.

narrow interests - means being especially interested in only one or two certain things, like numbers or computers or reptiles. People with autism sometimes get preoccupied with their narrow interests and spend a lot of time thinking and talking about them.

perseverate - means to keep doing the same things again and again, like getting stuck on playing one certain song, or asking the same question, over and over. This is common in people who have autism.

Pervasive Developmental Disorder (PDD) - is another name sometimes used to mean autism, usually when a person has mild or high-functioning autism.

rigid routines - are following a certain schedule or doing something a certain way that gets repeated the exact same way every time. (For example, always having to get dressed first before you can brush you hair in the morning). People with autism usually have certain routines they like to follow.

sensory problems - means when a person has problems using one or more of their senses - like seeing, hearing, taste, touch, and smell - to respond to the world all around them the way that most people do. Most people with autism have sensory problems. Sometimes they don't like loud noises, crowds, bright lights or being touched.

social skills - means knowing how to get along with other people, make friends, and figure out how to behave with people in different situations. People with autism need to be taught social skills that most other people learn naturally on their own.

stereotyped behavior - means certain repetitive things that persons with autism sometimes do like rocking back and forth or flapping their hands in the air. Children with autism may do these things when they get too excited or because it feels good.

DISCUSSION QUESTIONS FOR PARENTS AND CHILDREN

The following series of questions are offered as a starting point for parents, other family members, counselors, or therapists to use with children to help them begin to talk and express their feelings regarding their brother or sister with autism. These questions are intended only as a guide to assist parents (or others) and children to get started with sharing and understanding their feelings, and may be modified to fit the needs of the individual reader.

What kinds of things were confusing or difficult to understand about (your brother/sister) or his/her behavior before you learned about autism? Now that you know about autism, do you think that you understand him/her better? Are there things that he/she does that make more sense to you now? Do you have any more questions about ways that children with autism think, feel and behave?

How old do you think you were when you first realized that (your brother/sister) was different from you and most other kids? How did you figure this out? In what ways did you think he/she was different? What did he/she do or say, or how did he/she act, that seemed different to you than regular kids?

Tell me about a time when you felt embarrassed by (your brother/sister)? What happened?

Tell me about a time when you felt mad or frustrated with (your brother/sister). What happened?

Tell me about some times when you felt happy and proud of (your brother/sister).

Tell me about some times when (your brother/sister) really made you laugh. What did he/she do? What happened?

What are some ways that you have tried to help yourself deal with difficult feelings (sad, mad, etc.)? What works the best or helps you the most? Are there ways that I can help you when you are feeling upset?

What are some things that cause (your brother/sister) to feel mad or unhappy or worried? When he/she is feeling worried, how do you know it? What happens when you try to help him/her with his/her feelings?

Are there ways that you help other people to understand (your brother/sister)? What do you do when other people don't understand what (your brother/sister) says or wants?

What do you think are (your brother/sister's) special or unique abilities? What is he/she really good at? What do you especially like or enjoy about him/her? What has he/she been able to achieve? Have you helped him/her with this in any way?

Tell me about what happens when you and (your brother/sister) play together. What games does he/she know or like to play? Are any especially hard for him/her? Are there any games or activities that he/she is especially good at? When do you have the most fun together?

Are there things that make you worry about (<u>your brother/sister</u>)? Such as other kids teasing him/her, or he/she getting lost? Who do you talk to about your worries?

How do you think having a brother or sister who has autism has changed your family? Has it changed you in any way? Has it made you more sensitive or understanding about certain things having a family member with autism?

SELECTED RESOURCES FOR FURTHER INFORMATION

1. <u>Autism Society of America, Inc.</u> (ASA)
   7910 Woodmont Ave, Suite 650
   Bethesda, MD 20814
   (1-800-328-8476)

2. <u>Future Horizons, Inc</u>.
   721 W. Abram St.
   Arlington, TX 76013
   (800-489-0727 for mail-order materials and conferences on autism)
   www.futurehorizons-autism.com

3. <u>Sensory Resources, LLC</u>
   2200 E. Patrick Lane, Unit 3A
   Las Vegas, NV 89111
   (888-357-5867 for mail-order materials on sensory dysfunction)

4. <u>Autism Society of North Carolina</u>
   3300 Women's Club Drive
   Raleigh, NC 27612-4811
   (919-571-8555 for mail-order service for books on autism)

5. <u>Indiana Resource Center for Autism</u>
   Institute for the Study of Developmental Disabilities
   2853 E. 10th St.
   Bloomington, IN 47408-2601
   (812-855-6508 for mail-order materials on autism)

6. The <u>Morning News</u>
   c/o Carol Gray
   2140 Bauer Road
   Jenison, MI 49428
   (616-457-8955 for quarterly newsletter)